W9-AMN-840

How Do You Know It's Summer?

By Allan Fowler

Consultants:
Robert L. Hillerich, Ph.D., Bowling Green
State University, Bowling Green, Ohio

Mary Nalbandian, Director of Science,
Chicago Public Schools, Chicago, Illinois

Fay Robinson, Child Development Specialist

Eau Claire District Library

CP CHILDRENS PRESS ®
CHICAGO

105790

Design by Beth Herman Design Associates

Library of Congress Cataloging-in-Publication Data

Fowler, Allan
    How do you know it's summer? / by Allan Fowler.
        p. cm. –(Rookie read-about science)
        Summary: Presents such signs of summer as heat, playtime,
    thunderstorms, growing, and fun.
        ISBN 0-516-14923-2
        1. Summer–Juvenile literature. [1. Summer.] I. Title.
    II. Series: Fowler, Allan. Rookie read-about science.
QB637.6F69 1992
508–dc20   91-35061
                                                     CIP
                                                      AC

Copyright 1992 by Childrens Press®, Inc.
All rights reserved. Published simultaneously in Canada.
Printed in the United States of America.
    4 5 6 7 8 9 0 R 00 99 98 97 96 95 94

How do you know it's summer?

When the sun shines so hard that you think,

"It was never this hot before!"...

when grass and trees look greener than ever...

and you see flowers
everywhere, in every
color you can imagine...

when you're ready for bed,
but it's still daylight...

then you know it's
summertime!

10

Fruits and vegetables grow quickly in the warm sun.

Eau Claire District Library

You don't go to school in summer.

That leaves more time to play outside,

except during summer
storms when there might
be thunder and lightning.

Some boys and girls go away to summer camp.

Others take trips with their families.

They visit the beach...

or camp out in the
woods...

or travel to exciting new places.

You can also have lots
of summer fun without
going anywhere.

You might find you can do things you couldn't do last summer.

You can run faster.

You can swim better.

The 4th of July is a big summer holiday...

with picnics, parades, and
fireworks.

Summer is lots of fun.

But if it were always summer...wouldn't you miss the other times of the year?

Words You Know

summer

summer storm

lightning

farmer

fruit

vegetables

playing

picnic

parade

fireworks

Index

About the Author

Allan Fowler is a free-lance writer with a background in advertising. Born in New York, he lives in Chicago now and enjoys traveling.

Photo Credits

Photri – ©John R. McCauley, 31 (bottom right)

Photo Edit – ©Robert Brenner, 5; ©Myrleen Ferguson, 15, 18; ©Tony Freeman, 14, 17, 24, 31, (top left); ©Deborah Davies, 22; ©Richard Hutchings, 29; ©Elena Rooraid, 31 (top right)

Valan – ©Dr. A. Farquhar, Cover; ©Kennon Cooke, 6, 9, 30, (bottom right); ©Tom W. Parkin, 7; ©Pierre Kohler, 10; ©Joyce Photographics, 12, 30 (bottom left); ©A. Scullion, 13; ©Y.R. Tymstra, 16, 30 (top right); ©Ian Davis–Young, 20; ©Ken Patterson, 21; ©Tony Joyce, 25; ©R. LaSalle, 26, 31 (bottom left); ©Phillip Norton, 27; ©Michael J. Johnson, 30 (center right); ©Wilf Schurig, 30 (top left)

COVER: Looking at flowers

Eau Claire District Library